JOY AFTER FIFTY

For Bette,
    With love and
  joyful blessings,
      Connie

JOY AFTER FIFTY

A Woman's Guide to Passion, Purpose and Lasting Happiness

CONNIE CLARK

Hudson
View Press

Hudson View Press
369-B Third Street #106
San Rafael, CA 94901
1-800-996-4006
connie@joyafterfifty.com
www.joyafterfifty.com

Unattributed quotations are by Connie Clark

Printed in the United States of America
First Printing, 2011

ISBN: 978-0-9836871-0-8

Cover design by 1106 Design, LLC
Interior by 1106 Design, LLC
Cover photograph by Karen Schneider

Limits of Liability and Disclaimer of Warranty
The information in this book is intended to be educational and not for diagnosis, prescription or treatment of any medical or psychological disorder. The reader should consult with a physician or licensed psychotherapist in all matters relating to her or his mental health and, especially, with regard to symptoms that may require diagnosis or medical attention.

I dedicate this book to the memory of my mother, Bertie: Your dazzling smile invited us into your heart, where we found abiding love, support and friendship.

and

To women everywhere:

"Ever since happiness heard your name, it has been running through the streets trying to find you."

~ HAFIZ

Gratitude

*A*s with any creative endeavor, the seeds of *Joy after Fifty* were planted and fertilized by myriad inner and outer benevolent forces. It is with great pleasure that I express my gratitude to you all.

I am indebted to Patch Adams, MD, for igniting the spark for this book and for my creation of JoyWorks™ programs. In spite of your celebrity status, you showed up in 2001 at a high school gymnasium in Terra Linda, California, where you transformed the space and the participants into a state of pure delight. Thank you for legitimizing joy!

Woven into every page of this book is the wisdom and inspiration of countless women teachers, mentors, and authors who have taught about and/or modeled for me the way of the true feminine—spirited, creative, wise, nurturing, loving, and powerful! My deep gratitude to Angeles Arrien, PhD; Jean Houston, PhD; Marianne Williamson; Maria Shriver; Clarissa Pinkola Estes, PhD; Jean Shinoda Bolen, MD; Mary Manin Morrissey; Joan Borysenko, MD; Barbara Marx Hubbard; Elinor Gadon, PhD; and Lynn Twist.

To the leaders in the fields of positive psychology, neuropsychology, and the "science of happiness"—your research and writings have contributed greatly to this book and to my work. I offer my respect and gratitude to Martin Seligman, PhD; Ed Diener, PhD; Sonja Lybormirsky, PhD; Barbara Fredrickson, PhD; Stefan Klein, PhD; Jonathan Haidt; Kay Redfield Jamison, PhD; Dachner Keltner, PhD; and Tal Ben-Shahar, PhD.

I could not have written this book without the support of those whose "magic" opened a portal to bliss and divine creativity—you never failed to "deliver": Mother Nature; Mary Oliver; Jai Uttal; Krishna Das; and Jennifer Berezen.

To my bigger-than-life father, Hugh Todd Clark, who gave me the "grist" for this book and an ear for inviting language. You were a master of creative expression.

There are no words to adequately express how grateful I am for the love and support of my sister Dale; my brother Hugh; my aunt Audrey; and to all my treasured friends. You believed in me, encouraged me and made it possible for me to write this book joyfully!

To all my ancestors for lighting the path for me to follow.

Heartfelt appreciation and respect to my editors: To Joan Kirsner, for your expertise in creating a polished final manuscript. To Lin Ivice, for your enthusiastic support and effective "word doctoring." To Linda Jay Geldens, for your eagle eye as a proofreader.

And last, but not least, to all my readers: thank you for making the world a better place by living and working joyfully. We need your light and love!

"From Joy all beings are born,
By Joy they are sustained,
And into Joy they again return."

—TAITTIRIYA UPANISHAD

An Invitation

"Those who learn the secret to activating
inner joy will flourish."

You are so busy. Yet, you've taken time to pick up this book. This tells me that, in spite of all the activities and commitments in your life, you yearn for something more. Maybe it's time to invite more *joy* into your life.

You see, even though we've never met, you and I are connected. After living five decades or more, we know what it is to rejoice, laugh, love, create, celebrate, and grieve, as women. We are bonded by our common heritage and privilege as women who have reached the most powerful time of our lives—our 50s, 60s, 70s, 80s, and beyond. We may look very different on the outside. Some of us wear business suits, others jeans, sundresses, or saris. Whether single, coupled, separated, divorced, or widowed, no matter which continent we inhabit, we are guardians of a priceless treasure—the capacity to love and to nurture, to facilitate and collaborate, to experience and share joy.

As contemporary women over 50, we are more educated, gainfully employed and empowered than our foremothers. We have become breadwinners, homeowners, business

1

owners, artists, CEOs, and heads of state! These are great advancements, so why is it that...

WOMEN ARE UNHAPPIER
THAN EVER BEFORE!

We are living in an era of unprecedented stress. Natural disasters, global unrest, climate change, economic downturns, violence and terrorism, are just a few of the serious issues we face. If this isn't enough, life has become fast-paced, demanding, unpredictable and often exhausting.

Women are becoming "multitasking mavens" in an effort to keep up with society's heart-pounding pace. Many women suffer the adverse effects of this, which is further exacerbated by "techno-stress." Though not yet in the dictionary, the term "techno-stress" has been coined to describe the modern malady caused by information overload and a 24/7 demand to respond to e-mail, voicemail, and text messages. Ever wonder why the lines for lattes are so long? Increasingly, *we are becoming wired and tired! Are we doing more and loving life less?*

MY WAKE-UP CALL

One morning I was jolted awake by a dream, one of those dreams that leaves you feeling "God" has just whispered—maybe even shouted—in your ear. Imagine this:

I was seated in a small car, parked beside a vast, open field. Through the window, I watched a procession of "Polar Bear Women"—hundreds of women with human faces but furry polar-bear bodies. They were bent over in exhaustion, as they trudged slowly to some unknown destination. Their hair was dull and dry, their faces worn and haggard, their life force dim. I was horrified and terribly disturbed by their suffering.

As I awakened and mulled over this dream, I was overcome by a deep sense of sadness. I knew the dream was full of symbols depicting how women's joy, vitality, brilliance and potential are dangerously threatened by the rapid pace and burdensome stressors of these times.

YOUR WAKE-UP CALL

As women, we are inherently endowed with the power to give birth—to children, books, businesses, gardens, communities. Just think: If we could harness all the wisdom and life experiences of women over 50, we could rock our world—firmly, but gently—back onto an axis of harmony, peace and loving kindness. His Holiness the Dalai Lama has said that Western women will save the world. I would respectfully add that this potential extends beyond the West to all women on the planet, if given the opportunities and knowledge to keep our spirits joyful and strong!

The truth is that the world needs our gifts—now as never before! We all have a calling and a purpose in this lifetime. Whether it's to lovingly shape the lives of our children and grandchildren, to launch a new business, write our memoirs, or help build schools for girls in Afghanistan, as women 50+ the time has arrived for you and me to step fully into the life we were born to live.

Remember, you are a unique and powerful woman. There never has been and never will be anyone quite like you. And, it is truly your time to shine! This is the prime of your life. If you're a mom, the kids are most likely more independent now or have left the nest. It's also likely that you care less about what people think, and you feel freer to speak your mind and express your authentic self.

Now is the time to listen to the whispers of your soul. Before reading another word, ask yourself: *What is calling me at this time in my life? What would bring me joy and fulfillment?*

Women 50+ are "awakening" to persistent inner whispers of essential questions such as:

- Who am I now?
- Why was I born?
- What's next for me?
- Am I living from my "true nature", my most authentic self?
- Are there songs inside of me that are yet unsung?
- How well have I learned to shift from fear, control and negativity to love, acceptance and peace?
- What legacy will I leave for my children, grandchildren and future generations?
- What inner calling do I need to honor in order to have peace and fulfillment at the end of my life?

Here's the first of many secrets that you will discover in this book: *Whatever vision is beckoning to you, your success in that endeavor—even the realization of what it is—does not depend entirely on how hard you strive for it. Rather, it's contingent upon your ability to access inner joy. Those who learn the secrets of activating joy will flourish.*

THE FACTS ABOUT JOY

*"An investment in joy is the precursor
to all life's riches."*

Recent research in the fields of neuropsychology and positive psychology—referred to as the "science of happiness"—has proven that happier people enjoy more:

- LOVE
- HEALTH
- WEALTH
- ENERGY
- CREATIVITY
- CONFIDENCE
- CONCENTRATION
- PRODUCTIVITY
- INNER PEACE
- LONGEVITY

WHY I WROTE THIS BOOK

As I searched my heart, and later, the shelves of libraries and bookstores, I discovered the need for a book—especially for women over 50—dedicated to revealing the secrets to living a zesty, joyful life. As I imagined it, this book would be both inspirational and practical.

This book is my gift to you. It is the culmination of six decades of learning, in both academia and in life, how to be happy regardless of external conditions. It is based on scientific research, my experience and the experiences of hundreds of clients and friends who have been such a gift to me. I hope you, in turn, will pass it on as a gift to the women you love.

Professionally, for 25 years as a licensed psycho-therapist and the founder of JoyWorks™ programs (*www.connieclarkjoyworks.com*), I have been blessed to assist in the flourishing of hundreds of women—in my private practice, through coaching, in seminars, support groups, at women's conferences and, internationally, at my "*Spa for the Spirit*" retreats.

My clients come to me with issues ranging from depression, anxiety, grief, the loss of meaning, relation-ship difficulties, career and transition challenges, as well as addictive and compulsive disorders. I am so grateful to have witnessed the rebirth of joy, confidence, self-love and creativity, as my clients master the very principles you will find in this book.

However, the seeds for this book have actually been germinating since my childhood. My mother was a friendly, vivacious, loving woman. People would light up in her presence. She had such a youthful spirit, that when we went shopping together the local grocer would say, "Here come the Clark sisters!" No one would have guessed her secret: She was a battered woman.

As a child, I lived in terror of the nightly violence, which would send me running to protect her. I grew up handicapped with shame, low self-esteem and insecurity. As is common in children of alcoholics, I grew up feeling somehow bad, tainted, and unworthy. I dreaded speaking up in school and silently yearned for friends and a sense of belonging.

Through pure grace, I became fiercely determined to find happiness, in spite of my anxiety and sadness. With this determination, I discovered that I could activate a state of joy and well-being by immersing myself in the natural wonderland of the Connecticut forests, listening to music, dancing in my room to Tchaikovsky's "Waltz of the Flowers," losing myself in fairytales, or swimming off the beaches of Long Island Sound.

Thankfully, I also had allies along the way. As we walked the path to the Hudson River, my maternal grandmother taught me to rejoice in the face of a flower or the softness of a pussy willow. My paternal grandmother was a talented storyteller. She sparked my imagination with tales in which I starred and triumphed as the main character. As I write this, I am welling up with gratitude for the love of these two women who rescued my waning spirit and restored my happiness.

WHAT MAKES THIS BOOK DIFFERENT

I want you to have access to the secrets of living a joyful life, in a practical format that you can actually use to achieve **real results.** For that reason, *Joy after Fifty* is designed with your busy lifestyle in mind.

If you're like me, you don't have time to digest volumes of literature about the history and theory of a topic. You look for books that make it EASY for you to *absorb* and *apply* important information.

What you will find in this book:

A simple, step-by-step, 1-2-3 system designed for you, with instructions that are proven to get results.

It includes:

- A comprehensive system of proven practices, derived from psychology, neuropsychology, spiritual practices and ancient wisdom traditions.
- A simple, weekly program that conditions your mind, emotions and spirit for joy.
- 52 tested principles for activating joy in any circumstance.
- 208 provocative questions to increase the awareness essential for change and growth.
- 208 easy, manageable action steps for breakthrough results.
- A more joyful way of living, no matter what!

HOW TO USE THIS BOOK
FOR THE BEST RESULTS

Here are some suggestions for getting the most from the *Joy After Fifty* guide:

- **Invest in a beautiful journal** that makes your heart sing.
- Use the journal to **record responses to the weekly sections: Reflecting on Joy, Activating Joy and Deepening Joy.** Record insights, intuitive guidance, and intentions in the journal, as well.

- Create **a sacred space** for your weekly reflection and journaling.
- Light a candle, close your eyes and *feel* **your intention** to use *Joy after Fifty* as a guide to more happiness and aliveness. Imagine how your life, a year from now, might be different.
- Write your first journal entry by **stating your intention** for using this book. Record your thoughts about how your life might be different a year from now.
- If possible, **set a specific day** and time for using the program.
- **Record** the day and time in your appointment calendar.
- **Protect this time.** Turn off your phone and shut down your computer.
- Consider aligning with an **"accountability partner"** for mutual support or use the book to inspire a monthly women's circle.
- **Contact** Connie Clark for customized coaching and consultation: *connie@joyafterfifty.com.*
- **Visit** Connie's blog, *www.joyafterfifty.com,* to facilitate the mastery of joy principles and to read inspiring posts—dedicated to second half of life.
- **Sign up** at *www.joyafterfifty.com* to get the **Joy after Fifty newsletter:** information, inspiration, retreat announcements, and links to great research and references for women 50+.

MY PROMISE TO YOU

Imagine this: *By the end of this book, you will know exactly how to reap the benefits of a treasure chest of valuable gems from the fields of "positive psychology," "the psychology of women," "cognitive psychology" and "the science of happiness." You will have accessed life-enhancing practices from perennial spiritual traditions and women's wisdom ways.*

The following are 20 of the transformational effects of joy that have manifested for others. Imagine how your life would be different if you could:

1. Give yourself permission to prioritize joy.
2. Wake up with enthusiasm and inner peace.
3. Alleviate anxiety and depression.
4. Silence the inner critic.
5. Heal the toxicity of resentment, blame and judgment.
6. Rewire your brain to shift from fear to trust and courage.
7. Improve concentration and brain function.
8. Increase energy, vitality, and productivity.
9. Access intuitive guidance for effective decision-making.
10. Increase self-love and self-esteem.
11. Attract more love and friendship.
12. Enjoy mental, emotional, physical health and longer life.
13. Discover what you deeply desire for the rest of your life.
14. Eradicate self-defeating beliefs and inner voices.

15. Integrate new self-affirming, empowering beliefs.
16. Bring harmony to significant relationships.
17. Eliminate scarcity thinking.
18. Expect the best from life.
19. Embrace your true calling and heart's desire.
20. Know peace and fulfillment at the end of your life.

Week One

Welcome to a year of living joyfully as you discover the secrets to a happier you, regardless of your life's challenges. Joy is an innate gift and your birthright. Just as you were born with the capacity for reading and writing, you were born with the capacity for happiness. In order to activate this inborn gift, there are skills that can easily be learned and mastered. Scientific research shows that 40% of your joy is the result of implementing attitudes and actions—like those you will find in this book—that are proven to awaken happiness.

Reflecting on Joy

❀ What actions in my life are joy boosters/joy busters?

❀ What attitudes do I hold that increase/decrease my joy?

❀ In my lifetime, where have I invested money, time and effort in order to learn something new? For example: fitness training, cooking lessons, foreign-language classes, or doggie obedience training.

❀ Is it a good investment for me to commit time and energy in order to be happier?

 *Activating Joy*

1. It's a new day! You are embarking on a journey of self-love. If you follow the suggestions in the "Activating Joy" and "Deepening Joy"sections of this book, you will be absorbing and integrating myriad tools and skills proven to empower the capacity for generating joy. Congratulations for taking the first step!

2. As with any worthy endeavor, starting with a clear intention ensures a positive outcome! Define your intention for using this book.

3. In a special space that you have dedicated for using this program, sit quietly. Light a candle. Close your eyes and visualize how your life will be different in 52 weeks once you have learned the secrets to activating joy.

4. In a brand-new journal, record your intention and what you imagine as you look ahead one year from now. Blessings on your journey!

～ Deepening Joy ～

What I am grateful for this week

_____

_____

_____

_____

_____

_____

_____

_____

Three things that went well this week

_____

_____

_____

_____

_____

_____

_____

Week Two

*J*oy is the new success! Research shows that happy people are more successful in all areas of life: love, work, health, wealth and creativity. Since happiness is the precursor to many of life's riches, it makes sense to put joy-boosting activities (meditation, singing, dancing, laughing and playing) at the top of your to-do list.

 *Reflecting on Joy*

❋ When did I stop making time to delight my spirit (e.g., dancing, singing, painting, traveling, cooking, walking in nature, etc.)?

❋ What do I prioritize in my life/work?

❋ Where does joy fit on my list of priorities?

❋ Knowing that prioritizing joy is putting the horse before the cart on the road to success, what activities do I need to do in order to reclaim joy and make it a priority?

 *Activating Joy*

1. In your journal, describe an exhilarating time when you were fully engaged in a delightful activity—something you no longer make time for.

2. Close your eyes and recall that memory in full detail—see, hear, touch, smell and taste it. Let your body and spirit feel the joy. Hold the feeling for 60 seconds.

3. Write a letter to yourself from a loving being who gives you full permission to reclaim joyful activities. S/he convinces you that, as you put happiness first, you and everyone whose lives you touch will benefit.

4. Decide what joy-enhancing activity you will make time for this week. It should be so en-joy-able that you would choose to do it (or an equally satisfying activity) again for a month, a year or...perhaps forever.

Deepening Joy

What I am grateful for this week

_____
_____
_____
_____
_____
_____
_____
_____

Three things that went well this week

_____
_____
_____
_____
_____
_____
_____

Week Three

*J*oy is a state of being. Even in times of anxiety, grief or confusion, the state of joy is available to those who learn how to access it. Just as one can be trained to master a talent, such as drawing, gourmet cooking or tennis, one can learn how to master scientifically proven practices—behaviors and attitudes—that enhance inner joy and peace. In this book, you will discover the scientific secrets that promote vitality and happiness.

Reflecting on Joy

❋ As a child, what happiness-enhancing "skills" did I learn/not learn from my parents and teachers?

❋ What is one action/behavior that activates my joy—no matter what?

❋ How would it benefit my life—my family, relationships, friends, career, creativity and health—if I learned how to be more joyful?

❋ Am I willing to commit time each week to truly integrate the tools in this book?

 *Activating Joy*

1. Do a "Google" search on the Internet for the science of happiness and positive psychology.

2. Check out the International Positive Psychology Association at *www.ippa.org*. Becoming a member of the association gives you access to newsletters, webinars and conferences that reveal a new body of vital research on how people can live richer, more meaningful, happier lives.

3. For expert mentoring on using proven secrets to happiness and life satisfaction, send an e-mail to *connie@joyafterfifty.com*.

4. For the latest tips, articles, and inspiration for flourishing as you age, subscribe to our women's blog: *www.joyafterfifty.com*. There is a free gift waiting for you there!

Deepening Joy

What I am grateful for this week

_____
_____
_____
_____
_____
_____
_____
_____

Three things that went well this week

_____
_____
_____
_____
_____
_____
_____
_____

Week Four

"*All who would win joy must share it; happiness was born a twin.*" Research supports the wisdom of this quote by the poet Lord Byron. Serving others is one of the most reliable ways to activate one's own joy, even in challenging times. Having a daily intention to radiate joy to others is key to elevating one's own happiness.

Reflecting on Joy

❀ How can I create an optimally joyful inner life, so I can share it with others?

❀ What do I need to let go of to better share joy? (e.g., resentment, anxiety, hurrying through life.)

❀ What will I do to enhance my own joy this week?

❀ Who are the people, known to me or not, I will shower with joy this week?

Activating Joy

1. Send a loving message of appreciation to three people this week. Be specific about what you most appreciate about them.

2. Set your intention to radiate joy to everyone this week, including the strangers who cross your path.

3. Ask three friends what brings them joy. Find a way to deliver joy to them in some form.

4. Make time for your own joy. Schedule at least one joy-boosting experience this and every week.

~ Deepening Joy ~

What I am grateful for this week

_____
_____
_____
_____
_____
_____
_____
_____

Three things that went well this week

_____
_____
_____
_____
_____
_____
_____

Week Five

*K*now what feeds your soul and lights up your spirit. Become a master of the experiences that move a current of joy throughout your being. Mindfully follow these guideposts, as you would travel a path that is illuminated by the light of the full moon on a dark night.

Reflecting on Joy

❀ When have I experienced a "current of joy" running through me as a result of engaging in life from the core of my soul?

❀ What do I need to change or release at this time, in order for that current to flow uninhibited?

❀ What is my soul yearning for now?

❀ What do I need to initiate in order to intensify the flowing current of joy in my life today?

 *Activating Joy*

1. Light a candle. Sit quietly, eyes closed, listening to a piece of inspiring, heart-opening music.

2. Ask, "What is my soul yearning for at this time? What will rejuvenate my spirit?" Listen for the response.

3. Record the responses, whatever the form (e.g., images, words, a felt sense).

4. This week, commit to follow through on one special impression that supports your soul's desire.

Deepening Joy

What I am grateful for this week

_____
_____
_____
_____
_____
_____
_____
_____

Three things that went well this week

_____
_____
_____
_____
_____
_____
_____

Week Six

*K*eeping the end of your life in mind is a helpful practice for ensuring ease and joy today. Getting in touch with what will really matter—what will bring you peace and a sense of fulfillment as you look back on your life—illuminates that which needs to be prioritized today.

 *Reflecting on Joy*

❀ What do I imagine will really matter to me at the end of my life?

❀ As I evaluate my activities today, what aspects would generate a regret-free life review and ultimate contentment?

❀ How might I reassess my priorities in this regard? Where do I need to direct more—and less—of my attention and energy?

❀ Where would I have to say "no" to make more time for what really matters?

Activating Joy

1. Consider this line from Mary Oliver's poem "When Death Comes." *"When it's over I want to say 'all my life I was a bride married to amazement.'"* Journal about the message it has for you.

2. If you had three years to live, what would you make a priority and start doing immediately? Who or what would you make more time for?

3. Considering what you did NOT identify in the step above, what can you do to eliminate activities or associations that don't contribute to your eventual peace and fulfillment?

4. The future is not promised to any of us. As you design your activities this week, keep the "end" in mind. For each item on your to-do list, ask, "How is this commitment of my time and energy contributing/not contributing to my overall life satisfaction and joy?"

Deepening Joy

What I am grateful for this week

_____

_____

_____

_____

_____

_____

_____

_____

Three things that went well this week

_____

_____

_____

_____

_____

_____

_____

_____

Week Seven

Today's endless to-do-list lifestyle makes it so easy to get lost in multi-tasking and to lose track of the precious desires and visions that enrich one's life. Joyful lives are created by making time to nourish and manifest those visions. In today's rush-to-the-finish-line, beat-the-clock world, it is so easy to get off-track and lose sight of what really matters—the precious desires and visions that inspire and enliven us.

Reflecting on Joy

❀ Do I frequently multi-task in order to keep up?

❀ Am I losing track of the big picture of my life?

❀ What dream(s) for my life has gone dormant because I have been too busy?

❀ At this time of my life, what really matters?

Activating Joy

1. Make time to be still. Sit quietly, close your eyes and recall a deeply meaningful vision you have for your best life. See yourself fully engaged in that vision.

2. Activate all five senses as you imagine your best life. Feel the joy of living this dream. Amplify the feeling of joy for 60 seconds.

3. Draw, paint, sculpt or write about what really matters in your life.

4. To prevent losing sight of what you desire, ask a special person to become an "accountability partner." Schedule a regular time—weekly or monthly—to discuss how you are being true to what matters most in your precious life.

Deepening Joy

What I am grateful for this week

_____
_____
_____
_____
_____
_____
_____

Three things that went well this week

_____
_____
_____
_____
_____
_____
_____
_____

Week Eight

*R*e-enchant your life! Gaze at the moon. Wish on a star. Be amazed by the awe-inspiring beauty of a rose, an egret, a quiet lake. Stop. Breathe in the wonder all around you. Open your heart in gratitude for the magnificence of this life. Surely joy will fill your days.

Reflecting on Joy

❋ In my busy life, am I missing the wonder and the beauty all around me—a crescent moon, the setting sun, dew-drops on a blade of grass?

❋ Do I make time for the simple joy of being exquisitely present—with a flower, a child's smile, a juicy strawberry, a starry night?

❋ What memory can I recall of such total presence and gratitude?

❋ How would it impact my life to regularly pause in celebration of the "amazement" all around me?

Activating Joy

1. This week, practice being deliberately present with all the magnificence you encounter.

2. Allow yourself to be awed by the food on your plate, a sunrise, your lover's eyes, the sensation of a gentle touch, the fragrance of a flower.

3. Upon awakening, gently touch your body, appreciating it as a glorious gift—your eyes, ears, lips, hands, legs. Send your body waves of gratitude. Bless a new body part each day. Consider how your body has served you—all your life.

4. Create a ripple effect. Encourage loved ones, especially the children in your life, to be present with one of life's glorious gifts. Whether you invite them to be grateful for their miraculous body, a spectacular sunset, a magnificent flower, or a bird's serenade, awaken them to awe and wonder.

~ Deepening Joy ~

What I am grateful for this week

_____
_____
_____
_____
_____
_____
_____
_____

Three things that went well this week

_____
_____
_____
_____
_____
_____
_____
_____

Week Nine

An absolutely essential ingredient for a joyful life is self-love. Just as though we are in relationship with a best friend, treating ourselves with respect, patience and kindness is the key to inner harmony. Being gentle, accepting, and nurturing are three ways to approach ourselves with love. Making "dates" with ourselves for fun, laughter, relaxation, and inspiration is an effective way to deepen self-love and inner peace. As we practice self-love, our capacity to love others expands.

Reflecting on Joy

❀ Can I identify the inner blocks to loving myself? What are the beliefs, attitudes and habits that inhibit my self-love? Will I release them for good?

❀ On a scale of one to ten, with ten being the most loving, how would I rate my self-love? What would raise my score?

❀ If I were to treat myself as I would a lover, what actions would I take? What has kept me from taking these actions?

❀ What joyful past experiences have I gifted myself but have ceased doing? Why?

 *Activating Joy*

1. Set your intention to actively practice self-love. This week, keep a log of all the ways in which you are loving toward yourself through actions and thoughts.

2. Take an inventory of all your strengths, accomplishments and positive qualities. List them in your journal.

3. This week, read the above list upon awakening and/or before going to sleep each night. With your hands over your heart, say to yourself, *"I Love you!"*

4. Treat yourself to at least one hour of nurturing this week. In doing so, you demonstrate that you deserve care and tenderness. Ideas include a massage, a facial, a walk in nature and taking time to dance, sing, and play...or do *nothing*!

～ Deepening Joy ～

What I am grateful for this week

_____

_____

_____

_____

_____

_____

_____

Three things that went well this week

_____

_____

_____

_____

_____

_____

_____

Week Ten

"Don't Postpone Joy," as the bumper sticker says. Those who prioritize joy flourish. Research shows that making time to play is essential to creativity, concentration and clarity of purpose. Adding joy to your calendar is not frivolous, but a necessary action for optimal human functioning.

Reflecting on Joy

❋ What judgments or restrictions do I have about prioritizing joy? Where did I learn them?

❋ What obligations or "shoulds" cause me to postpone my joy?

❋ If anything was possible, and I had abundant time, what five joy-enhancing experiences would I create?

❋ Take a look at your weekly joy-meter. Do you have enough joy in your life to function optimally?

 *Activating Joy*

1. Make a list of all the people or things that "cause you" to postpone joy.

2. Recite daily this affirmation. *"I faithfully prioritize my joy for the highest good of all concerned."*

3. Of the five joy-enhancing activities or practices you identified, commit to pursuing one (or more) of them this week.

4. Shower yourself with love and gratitude for making time for joy. Repeat consistently!

Deepening Joy

What I am grateful for this week

_____

_____

_____

_____

_____

_____

_____

Three things that went well this week

_____

_____

_____

_____

_____

_____

_____

Week Eleven

"*Joy is not a pie-in-the-sky ideal! It comes from deliberate actions you take to create a joyful state of being.*" These words of wisdom come from Jan Wahl, San Francisco's favorite movie critic, film historian, and sought-after speaker. Knowing that films have a powerful impact on our emotions, Jan encourages us to watch joy-inducing movies to lift our spirits. Such movies (a) give us someone to root for—we share in the delight of their successes (e.g., Cool Runnings; The Full Monty; City Island; The Pursuit of Happyness) (b) appeal to the spirit of the best and highest in us (e.g., Whale Runner; Pay It Forward; It's a Wonderful Life) (c) portray women in roles which demonstrate their assertiveness and authenticity, their adventures and triumphs (e.g., Harold and Maude; Fried Green Tomatoes; It's Complicated; Julie and Julia; Shirley Valentine).

Reflecting on Joy

❋ Recall one of your favorite movies. Considering how movies evoke strong emotions, what do you remember feeling (sadness, courage, excitement, fear)? Why do you suppose that movie had an impact on your psyche?

❋ Who were your favorite actors/actresses as a child? What did they represent to you? And today?

❋ What role in a movie would you have liked to play, as a child/adult? Why?

❋ If you were "Queen of the Film Industry," what kinds of movies would you produce for women 50+ in these times? What themes would be prominent in your films?

Activating Joy

1. Plan a fun Women's Film Fest! Invite friends to a double feature of one or two films from (c) above. Share yummy snacks as you discuss how each of you was impacted by the qualities of the women cast in the leading roles. Discuss how your lives would be different if you were to emulate those qualities.

2. In your journal, record the ways in which you were affected by the women's roles in the films you watched at your gathering.

3. Name three qualities, attitudes, or behaviors of the leading ladies that would positively impact your life at this time. Write each on a sticky note and post where you'll see it daily (e.g., the bathroom; on the ceiling over your bed; in the kitchen).

4. Write about how your life might be different if you were to emulate those three qualities. Choose one specific desire or goal and, acting "as if" you embody those qualities, make a 6–12 month plan to make that dream real! Hire a mentor/coach to whom you can be accountable and you will achieve your desires.

~ Deepening Joy ~

What I am grateful for this week

_____

_____

_____

_____

_____

_____

_____

_____

Three things that went well this week

_____

_____

_____

_____

_____

_____

_____

Week Twelve

*I*n times of doubt and confusion, consider the words of Lao-tzu from the Tao Te Ching: *"Do you have the patience to wait till the mud settles and the water is clear? Can you remain unmoving till the right action arises all by itself?"* When stuck in a holding pattern, know that a solution is waiting for the perfect moment to be born. Create inner peace and contentment by remembering that "right action" will reveal itself to you at just the right time.

 *Reflecting on Joy*

❀ What current issue in my life or work is "muddy" and challenging my patience?

❀ How do I feel as I read the above quote?

❀ Does some aspect of Lao-tzu's sage advice alleviate my stress and impatience?

❀ How would it be different to relax and trust that clarity and right action will arise, that everything is happening in perfect timing?

Activating Joy

1. Write down a pressing issue about which you need more clarity. Sit quietly, reflecting on it and notice any tension that arises.

2. Create a ritual of release. Perform a symbolic action that demonstrates your willingness to trust and let go of the need to have clarity now. Examples include tearing up, burying or burning a symbol of the issue needing clarity. Perform this with great intention.

3. Post the following affirmation: *"Trusting that the right action is unfolding in perfect timing, I am peaceful and happy."*

4. Ask daily, in meditation or prayer, for guidance and clarity.

~ Deepening Joy ~

What I am grateful for this week

_____
_____
_____
_____
_____
_____
_____
_____

Three things that went well this week

_____
_____
_____
_____
_____
_____
_____

Week Thirteen

The company of other women is "good medicine" for the female body, mind and spirit. When women converse and connect, an extra dose of oxytocin—a feel-good hormone—is released. Women are reclaiming self-esteem and personal empowerment by participating in ongoing "circles." These circles are sanctuaries in which a woman can discover her authenticity, as she is "midwifed" into birthing her true nature and her unique voice.

Reflecting on Joy

✸ How did my relationship with my mother, or the absence of a mother, affect my current attitudes toward women?

✸ What aspects of being a woman have I, or have I not yet, accepted and embraced? Do they prevent me from embracing my womanhood and truly loving other women as friends and "sisters"?

✸ What experiences do I currently have with other women that intentionally foster deep connection, communication and empowerment?

✸ What women would I wish to include in an ongoing "circle" for support, guidance and loving connection?

Activating Joy

1. Light a candle. Close your eyes and breathe slowly and fully to ground yourself. Imagine yourself in a sacred women's lodge. You are surrounded by concentric circles of all your female ancestors, from all time.

2. Activate all your senses as you experience the depth of love and wisdom they are radiating to you now.

3. Formulate a question regarding a significant life issue. Present it to the women surrounding you. Listen carefully. Record their "responses."

4. This week, set aside time to imagine yourself creating a women's circle or rejuvenating an existing circle. Consider the who, what, where and how of your intention. For an individual or group coaching consultation on *"How To Create and Sustain A Vibrant Women's Circle"*, send an email to *connie@joyafterfifty.com*.

~ Deepening Joy ~

What I am grateful for this week

_____
_____
_____
_____
_____
_____
_____
_____

Three things that went well this week

_____
_____
_____
_____
_____
_____
_____

Week Fourteen

*A*s a woman in the second half of life, it's essential that you identify a life dream that makes your heart sing. Whether simple or grand, your burning desire, and a plan to achieve it, will reveal a pathway of deep joy. Your world will light up as you move in the direction of your dream…one goal, one action, one baby step at a time.

Reflecting on Joy

❋ What dream makes my heart sing at this time?

❋ When I imagine living my dream as though it is already happening, how do I feel?

❋ What inner qualities could I intentionally access to overcome any obstacles to realizing my dream (e.g., trust, courage, perseverance)?

❋ Knowing that it takes "a village" to help make one's dreams come true, who would make up my most powerful "dream team"? Examples include: a coach, a friend, a psychotherapist, an accountability partner.

Activating Joy

1. Set a timer for 12 minutes. Beginning with the phrase, *"My greatest desire at this time is…"* write nonstop until the time is up. Take more time if you wish. Reflect upon what you wrote. Does it surprise you? How does it feel?

2. Write down all the perceived inner and outer obstacles to fulfilling your desire. Close your eyes and activate your fierce intention to release the obstacles. Ask for support from a higher power of your choosing. With determination, burn the list. Give thanks. Tell a trusted person what you have released.

3. Commit fully to manifesting your desire. Write down your commitment to manifest your desire and the date by which you will have achieved it. Identify the actions you need to take to successfully fulfill the commitment.

4. Make a "vision board" of images that represent aspects of your dream. As you look daily at the images, pause and feel the joy of having your desire, as though it's happening right now. Expect success!

~ Deepening Joy ~

What I am grateful for this week

_____

_____

_____

_____

_____

_____

_____

_____

Three things that went well this week

_____

_____

_____

_____

_____

_____

_____

Week Fifteen

Sometimes our minds are like a bad neighborhood—dark and scary. It's essential to become aware of the shady characters—the inner critic, doomsayer, judge, pessimist, perfectionist, whiny child and internalized critical parent—who broadcast negativity. We must clean up the inner neighborhood and invite only friendly characters who broadcast positive thinking. Happiness and peace of mind increase as you dial into the frequency of affirming, loving, solution-oriented thoughts. Practicing "thought patrol" keeps the inner neighborhood conducive to joy!

Reflecting on Joy

❀ What inner demons rob me of my peace and joy? How are they criticizing, comparing, complaining, or whining?

❀ Am I aware of specific "self-talk" that comes from my inner critic, perfectionist, or pessimist?

❀ Knowing that it is within my power to transform disturbing thoughts and beliefs, how would my life be different if I learned to master my mind?

❀ What negative beliefs about myself or others would be most helpful to positively transform, starting this week?

Activating Joy

1. This week, practice "thought patrol." Keep a log of exactly what the inner critic, perfectionist or pessimist is broadcasting to you.

2. Practice "thought stopping." Say (like you mean it) "stop" or "cancel" to negativity. Reinforce a positive attitude by shifting the mind's focus to an image of a person or a pet that you love. Feel and amplify the love you have for them. Hold the feeling for at least 60 seconds.

3. To silence the inner critic, shower yourself with praise and gratitude this week. Start by writing at least ten things people like, appreciate, and respect about you.

4. Practice positive thinking. Look for the good in people and events, beginning with yourself. Each day this week, record all the good you see, even in the face of challenges.

~ Deepening Joy ~

What I am grateful for this week

_____

_____

_____

_____

_____

_____

_____

_____

Three things that went well this week

_____

_____

_____

_____

_____

_____

_____

_____

Week Sixteen

*I*n times of despair, know that happiness has not abandoned you. The Persian poet, Rumi, reminds us that, *"Out of a shattered heart emerges a fiery fountain of sacred passion that never runs dry."* The dark times are fertile ground for new growth, fresh inspiration and joyful purpose. Be gentle with yourself. Look for soothing moments: a bird's song, a cup of steaming tea, or the embrace of a loved one. Give yourself permission to retreat into little moments of joy.

Reflecting on Joy

✤ As I look back on my life, when was my heart shattered by loss?

✤ What new growth and/or purpose emerged from my despair?

✤ How do I feel about choosing to invite happiness, even in times of loss or sorrow?

✤ How might my grief or sadness be lessened by imagining an inner "fountain of sacred passion and a pool of joy?"

Activating Joy

1. Sit quietly and reflect about experiences—yours or another's—when, from out of the darkness, a new passion, purpose, or joy was birthed.

2. Record these experiences in your journal for encouragement and hope—to comfort a heavy heart, now and in the future.

3. Share Rumi's quote with someone you know who could use a little hope.

4. If you are now experiencing a dark time in your life:
   a. Post Rumi's quote and other encouraging expressions around your home.
   b. Be your own best friend. Schedule one action this week, and every week, that taps into your fountain of joy.
   c. Don't be isolated! Seek the support of professionals and loved ones.
   d. Smile! It nourishes the brain with happiness hormones.

~ Deepening Joy ~

What I am grateful for this week

_____
_____
_____
_____
_____
_____
_____
_____

Three things that went well this week

_____
_____
_____
_____
_____
_____
_____

Week Seventeen

*I*n this era of speed, intensity, information overload, the 24/7 demands of e-mail and text communication, and the resulting "techno-stress," a woman's health and spirit can be threatened. Ensuring joy after fifty today requires a daily program of intentional practices that calm the nervous system, optimize brain function, and restore overall balance. Custom-designing a personal "spiritual" practice is the key to flourishing in these challenging times.

 *Reflecting on Joy*

✳ What do I do in the first 30 minutes after awakening?

✳ Do those activities create the ideal inner condition for me to be my "best self" during the day? Why? Why not?

✳ How would my life be impacted if I started each day by sitting quietly, lighting a candle, reading a poem, singing, or moving to music instead of turning on the TV or checking e-mail?

✳ Where might I learn to meditate? How I can deepen my existing meditation practice?

Activating Joy

1. Record in your journal a description of your idea of the most beneficial way to ease into a new day. Include activities that have grounded and centered you in the past.

2. This week, research on the Internet or in the library some of the following practices that are shown to restore inner equilibrium, promote optimal health and functioning, and combat stress:
   a. Meditation—focusing on the breath, using a mantra, or focusing on a candle flame.
   b. Chanting—listen to Jai Uttal, Krishna Das and Deva Premal on iTunes.
   c. Brain wave entrainment: a process that can slow brain waves and relax the mind.

3. Initiate or enhance a daily centering practice. Within the first hour after awakening, experiment with one intentional activity from #2.

4. To ensure peak performance, health, and well-being, design a morning practice that best suits you. This week, observe the beneficial effects of starting each day by creating the optimal inner condition for flourishing. Take five-minute meditation breaks to refresh.

~ Deepening Joy ~

What I am grateful for this week

_____
_____
_____
_____
_____
_____
_____
_____

Three things that went well this week

_____
_____
_____
_____
_____
_____
_____

Week Eighteen

Forgiveness is an act of self-love that liberates us from the poisons of bitterness and resentment. To forgive a person, not necessarily the behavior, releases us from the heavy burden of the past, so that we can flourish today. Make a decision to release the toxicity of resentment by forgiving those who you feel have wronged you. Welcome in the sunshine of your spirit.

Reflecting on Joy

❋ Who in my life have I yet to forgive? Why?

❋ How is my inner experience/mood affected when I remember this person, this event?

❋ When I read this week's principle, am I more receptive to forgiving? Do I accept that I have more life force and freedom to be my most creative, happy self in doing so?

❋ Am I ready to set the intention to forgive, starting now?

 *Activating Joy*

1. Sit quietly, breathing slowly and deeply. On each in-breath say, *"I breathe in forgiveness."* On each out-breath say, *"I breathe out resentment, anger, hatred, or bitterness."* Repeat daily this week.

2. Forgive yourself first. Gently call to mind a mistake you made. Close your eyes. Imagine a radiant, golden light beaming love and forgiveness into your heart.

3. Imagine the face of someone you want to forgive. Send that radiant golden light of love and forgiveness into his or her heart. Say out loud "_____ (your name), *I forgive you.*" Take a deep breath and repeat.

4. Write a letter of forgiveness to this person, whether living or deceased. If the person is living, decide if sending the letter is for the highest good of all concerned.

Deepening Joy

What I am grateful for this week

_____
_____
_____
_____
_____
_____
_____
_____

Three things that went well this week

_____
_____
_____
_____
_____
_____
_____
_____

Week Nineteen

*H*appiness comes by honoring the needs of your soul. While the ego shouts its demands, you must move into stillness to hear the whisper of the soul. Loving yourself means making time to be still and nourish your soul—an essential ingredient in experiencing joy. In order to flourish in these times, you must initiate a "to-be" list to counter the demands of the almighty "to-do" list.

Reflecting on Joy

❋ What three people, three places, and three experiences nourish my soul?

❋ How am I demonstrating that I honor the care and nurturing of my soul?

❋ In the busyness of daily living, what joy-enhancing people, places or experiences have I neglected?

❋ What one person, one place and/or one experience will I reclaim this week, to honor and care for my soul? What will this look and feel like?

Activating Joy

1. Having identified the one person, place and/or experience above, commit to connecting with it in your weekly schedule.

2. In your journal, list the obstacles to making room in your life for nourishing your soul, whether it's beliefs, behaviors, work or relationships.

3. Close your eyes. Conjure up the faces of loved ones. Notice their love for you shining through their eyes. See, hear and feel them showering you with love and encouraging you to make time for yourself.

4. Schedule ten-minute daily breaks this week. Simply be still, pause, and refresh your spirit.

Deepening Joy

What I am grateful for this week

_____
_____
_____
_____
_____
_____
_____
_____

Three things that went well this week

_____
_____
_____
_____
_____
_____
_____
_____

Week Twenty

Not only is spending time in nature a free, fast-acting, scientifically proven antidote to stress, it also alleviates depression and improves decision making by rejuvenating the mind and relaxing the body. Not making time to retreat to a favorite nature spot is like having a magic happiness pill but refusing to swallow it. Nature calms the nervous system, while enhancing concentration and creative thought. Being in nature reawakens joy, wonder and inner peace—a true "spa for the spirit!"

Reflecting on Joy

❋ What are my favorite nature spots (e.g., the roaring ocean, a carpet of pine needles in the forest, a vast and colorful desert, a still mountain lake)?

❋ Knowing that being alone in nature reduces stress, restores the spirit and enhances joy, how am I availing myself of this free therapy?

❋ How will nourishing my soul have a ripple effect?

❋ Who else will benefit? How?

Activating Joy

1. This week, retreat to a favorite nature spot, even if you live in a city. Bring note cards and a pen. In advance, identify an issue or endeavor around which you are seeking clarity.

2. Enter the nature spot with reverence and gratitude. Pause. Close your eyes and ask for guidance about the issue you defined (e.g., any aspect of your life needing clarity and direction).

3. Next, release your request. Savor the beauty of the trees, the water, the sky, the creatures. Be amazed and delighted. Feel stress melting away. Celebrate calmness.

4. Make notes along the way of any intuitive guidance (e.g., words, images, songs) that arises. Offer thanks and repeat regularly!

~ Deepening Joy ~

What I am grateful for this week

_____
_____
_____
_____
_____
_____
_____
_____

Three things that went well this week

_____
_____
_____
_____
_____
_____
_____
_____

Week Twenty-One

Small acts of kindness have the power to warm the hearts of both the giver and the receiver. An unexpected smile, a friendly greeting, an offer to assist with groceries or pay another's toll can dramatically enhance the joy of everyone involved. Research has proven that engaging in acts of kindness is an effective way to increase happiness—so simple and so needed in today's world.

# Reflecting on Joy

✻ Do I remember a time when someone brightened my day with an unexpected act of kindness? How did it impact me?

✻ Who are the people outside of my family—merchants, co-workers, neighbors—I frequently encounter?

✻ What are three simple acts of kindness I could offer them?

✻ How would it affect my daily experience to consistently spread kindness to all beings I encounter?

 *Activating Joy*

1. Imagine yourself as a benevolent, generous being, whose mission is to spread loving-kindness to all.

2. Realizing the power you have to significantly brighten the lives of others in these difficult times, make a list of creative, yet simple, acts of kindness you can spread around your world.

3. This week, launch a new "mission" of radiating kindness. Starting today, make this a daily priority. Notice how your happiness is elevated as well.

4. Inspire others to spread kindness. Tell three friends, family members or co-workers about your "mission." Encourage them to do the same. And here's another idea: Initiate a "kindness campaign" at work!

Deepening Joy

What I am grateful for this week

_____
_____
_____
_____
_____
_____
_____
_____

Three things that went well this week

_____
_____
_____
_____
_____
_____
_____

Week Twenty-Two

"To find joy in work is to discover the fountain of youth," mused Pearl S. Buck. In 2011, Tony Hsieh, the wildly successful CEO of Zappos.com, Inc., advocates making happiness in the workplace a top priority as a path to prosperity. Shannon Roy, Crystal Mouzon and Patti Crowley are three Zappos women who are 50+ and know the benefits of working for a company that puts fun and happiness first. They are energized by the corporate culture that "feels like family" and is committed to delivering "WOW through service." Shannon, who says she is starting her "second and most fun life" at Zappos, is the manager of a department called PEACE, Love and Happiness! The mission of the department is to "ensure that, no matter how large the company expands, our culture will thrive—now and forever!" Imagine, if each of us—whether we are a CEO, a manager, an entrepreneur or retired—were guided by peace, love and happiness in all our endeavors!

Reflecting on Joy

❋ Whether as an employee or an entrepreneur, what work or projects have I engaged in that were as natural for me as breathing and that enhanced my joy and vitality?

❋ Is my current work/project feeding my joy and fulfillment, or fueling my stress?

❋ Are my work objectives about more than making money? Am I having fun? Am I inspired? If not, what changes do I need to consider?

❋ If anything were possible, what new work/project would I pursue for fun and prosperity?

Activating Joy

1. Be inspired. "Google": *zappos core values*. Read and reflect upon the 10 core values. Consider how your work or life projects would be affected by applying these values. Record thoughts in your journal.

2. Choose one of the Zappos core values to emulate this week. Write it on a large sticky note. Place it in a prominent place. For example, *"Be passionate and determined."* Apply the value to all your endeavors throughout the day.

3. To reinforce the value, speak aloud the affirmation: *"I am fulfilled and happy at my work/project as I practice being _____.* (insert core value: e.g.,"passionate and determined").

4. Choose a new core value for each of the next 10 weeks. Repeat steps 2 and 3 above with each core value. To see these values in action, if you can, arrange to have a tour of Zappos in Henderson, Nevada…unforgettable, fun and inspiring!

～ Deepening Joy ～

What I am grateful for this week

_____
_____
_____
_____
_____
_____
_____
_____

Three things that went well this week

_____
_____
_____
_____
_____
_____
_____

Week Twenty-Three

Get in touch with what you value in life. Your joy will be enhanced as you engage in the pursuit of what positive psychology calls "self-concordant" goals—endeavors that are in alignment with your strengths, your values and that make your heart sing. End the struggle to achieve any goal that diminishes your delight and inner peace.

Reflecting on Joy

※ What do I highly value in my life/work (e.g., family, creativity, achievement, community, solitude?)

※ As I review my adult life, what activities have brought me the most joy?

※ What values and/or personal strengths are inherent in those activities?

※ Which of my values and talents are/are not being honored or activated in my life today?

Activating Joy

1. Make a list of what you value most in your life/work (e.g., harmony, creativity, leadership).

2. Identify one key value that, if you made it a higher priority, would enhance your joy in work/life.

3. Describe, in writing, five ways you can prioritize this value. For instance, if you value loving relationships, you might send someone flowers, express gratitude, buy a gift, or call a loved one regularly.

4. Make a list of three to five goals you wish to achieve in the next six months or year. Be certain they are "self-concordant" goals, in alignment with your values and natural talents. Meet regularly with a coach or "accountability partner" to stay focused on your self-concordant goals.

Deepening Joy

What I am grateful for this week

_____

_____

_____

_____

_____

_____

_____

_____

_____

Three things that went well this week

_____

_____

_____

_____

_____

_____

_____

_____

Week Twenty-Four

*M*ary Oliver's poems, which revere nature and life, speak to the soul. They enliven the human spirit. From her poem "The Ponds" come these lines: *"Still what I want in my life is to be dazzled—to cast aside the weight of facts and maybe even to float a little above this difficult world. I want to believe I am looking into the white fire of a great mystery."* Reading a Mary Oliver poem upon awakening ignites a joyful spirit—an awe-inspiring way to start each day.

Reflecting on Joy

❀ With all of my responsibilities, to-do lists and challenges, has my life lost a bit of dazzle? In what ways?

❀ What reconnects me to a sense of wonder, awe, and enchantment?

❀ What have been the obstacles to my having more delight and wonder in my life?

❀ How can I rekindle joy and awe in my life this week and throughout this coming year?

Activating Joy

1. Decide that you will begin this week to reclaim or find anew that which dazzles and re-enchants your life.

2. Create an affirmation such as, *"I am full of joy, vitality and ease as I engage in experiences that re-enchant my life."*

3. Write in your journal starting with "I remember the feeling of wonder and delight when…" Pay attention to what is revealed.

4. Identify one action step you will take that adds brightness to your life this week. Repeat monthly throughout the next year. Celebrate a life of newfound wonder and boundless joy. Pass it on to all who cross your path.

~ Deepening Joy ~

What I am grateful for this week

_____

_____

_____

_____

_____

_____

_____

_____

_____

Three things that went well this week

_____

_____

_____

_____

_____

_____

_____

_____

Week Twenty-Five

*R*emember the bumper sticker, *"Don't believe every-thing you think"*? Since our thoughts create our feelings, negative thoughts can evoke doubt, fear, insecurity, resentment, anger, and anxiety. The stories that are fabricated in the mind determine whether we live in happiness or misery.

Reflecting on Joy

❋ What stories do I tell myself that inhibit my joy? For example: *"I'm too old"; "I don't have what it takes"; "I'm not pretty, smart or rich enough"; "If only I looked younger, lost weight, had more money...then I'd be happy!"*

❋ If I were to free up creative energy by abandoning these stories, what project, adventure, goal or cause would I be empowered to tackle?

❋ Am I seriously willing to protect my vital life force by eliminating these stories from my inner and outer conversations?

❋ What limiting story will I release first?

Activating Joy

1. Take an inventory of your joy-busting "stories." On a sheet of paper, or in your journal, record them under one of the following five headings: Career, Family, Friends, Home and Health.

2. If you are inspired to stop dissipating your energy with these joy-inhibiting stories, acknowledge your determination to give them up. With a strong intention to be free of them, burn the stories you've identified. Then, celebrate!

3. Post and recite daily this affirmation: *"I am worthy, powerful and lovable just by being who I am—free of limiting stories. I re-enchant my life with joy and inspiration."*

4. Observe how the media spins "stories" about the products or services you need to be happy, lovable, secure or successful. Challenge these stories as they invade your mind. This week, create a new "story" about the joys you have that are unrelated to "stuff."

Deepening Joy

What I am grateful for this week

_____
_____
_____
_____
_____
_____
_____
_____

Three things that went well this week

_____
_____
_____
_____
_____
_____
_____

Week Twenty-Six

The key to fulfillment and authentic success is to resist any inclination to design your life as a carbon copy of anyone else's. Your heart holds the secret blueprint for a life design that is a perfect reflection of your unique purpose and gifts. Having the courage to walk away from a life path meant for another is a wildly significant step toward new-found freedom and fulfillment.

Reflecting on Joy

❋ Who have I tried to emulate or imitate in life/work? Why?

❋ Apart from outside influences, do I know what my authentic path and true heart's calling is? If not, who could help me find clarity?

❋ How would I envision my life if I were to truly follow my heart? What would need to change?

❋ What empowers me to create my life as a unique expression of who I really am?

Activating Joy

1. Each morning this week, sit quietly for ten minutes with your eyes closed. Invoke a guide (e.g., ancestor, higher power, wise woman).

2. Ask: *"How can I more completely live my authentic life? What do I need to say yes or no to?"* Sit quietly and listen. Record responses, including images, words and intuitions.

3. Highlight the responses that make your heart sing.

4. Follow the joy! At the end of this week, choose one response that brings you joy. Tell a friend how you'll commit to activating it in your life. Celebrate being uniquely you! Revisit this exercise monthly.

Deepening Joy

What I am grateful for this week

_____
_____
_____
_____
_____
_____
_____
_____

Three things that went well this week

_____
_____
_____
_____
_____
_____
_____

Week Twenty-Seven

"You will succeed if you persevere, and you will find joy in overcoming obstacles," said Helen Keller, who was blind, deaf and mute. She was a master of overcoming multiple obstacles. Consider the fierce intention that empowered her resilience and happiness. Great inspiration and strength can be drawn from collecting and reading such words of wisdom.

 *Reflecting on Joy*

✻ On what important, though challenging, personal or professional issue do I need to persevere? Why?

✻ What obstacles appear to be in the way?

✻ What new, positive story can I tell myself for encouragement and resilience?

✻ Who can help me—a loved one, a coach, a psychotherapist, a circle of wise women?

Activating Joy

1. Write down the negative, pessimistic "stories" you tell yourself about this issue.

2. Create a new, hopeful, empowering story. Write it down. Read it daily this week. What would Helen Keller say to encourage you?

3. Visualize yourself succeeding. Most important, activate the attendant positive feelings—excitement and enthusiasm.

4. Standing with your eyes closed, see yourself after having overcome the challenge and engaging in some joyful experience as a result. This could be a celebration, a new job, a romance or a new home. Repeat throughout the week.

~ Deepening Joy ~

What I am grateful for this week

_____

_____

_____

_____

_____

_____

_____

_____

Three things that went well this week

_____

_____

_____

_____

_____

_____

_____

Week Twenty-Eight

"*Take a music bath once or twice a week for a few seasons. You will find it is to the soul what water is to the body.*" Oliver Wendell Holmes must have been listening to the music of singer/songwriter Karen Drucker...in another life! Karen's songs touch the heart and soul of women with a dose of laughter, inspiration, and encouragement—"good medicine" for us all in these challenging times! Karen radiates compassion, playfulness and love through her music. In her book, *Let Go of the Shore: Stories and Songs that Set the Spirit Free,* she shares some of her own secrets to activating joy. They include making a list of what brings her joy and making "joy dates" with herself. She also checks out her "joy meter" after engaging with people and asks herself, *"Did I feel alive and happy, or drained and feeling like I wanted to run for the hills?"* Listening to Karen's music will boost your vitality and happiness.

Reflecting on Joy

※ What music lifts me up and boosts my happiness?

※ How often do I make time to listen to that kind of music? Why? Why not?

※ What people, places, and/or things activate my joy/ drain my energy?

※ If I were to make "joy dates" with myself, what would I be doing?

 *Activating Joy*

1. This week, gift yourself with one (or more) of Karen Drucker's CDs. Check them out at *www.karen drucker.com*.

2. Listen to the CD this week—in your car, at the gym or at home. Sing along! Share it with women friends.

3. Make a list of what makes your heart sing, including people, places and experiences.

4. Follow Karen's examples and make a "joy date" with yourself from items in #3 above. Repeat weekly and watch your "joy meter" rise!

Deepening Joy

What I am grateful for this week

_____

_____

_____

_____

_____

_____

_____

_____

Three things that went well this week

_____

_____

_____

_____

_____

_____

_____

Week Twenty-Nine

*E*very aspect of life can be transformed, from the mundane to the sacred. When you view even the ordinary events and actions in your life as sacred, moments become infused with zest and meaning. This is how to re-enchant your life. Joy is the reward.

Reflecting on Joy

✤ Am I slowing down enough to see the sacred in the most ordinary objects, activities and people?

✤ What would it be like to transform an ordinary space at home into a sacred space where I sit to reflect, write, meditate? How can I enhance an existing sacred space?

✤ What experience or events have I participated in where the ordinary was transformed into the sacred? What was the process (a wedding, a funeral, a birth)?

✤ What daily activities that I perform habitually could be transformed into meaningful rituals (e.g., as I start my car, I feel it igniting my intention for the day)?

Activating Joy

1. Create a sacred space. Suggestions include an "altar," which can be as simple as a box covered with a beautiful fabric, upon which you place a candle and objects that you find sacred. Let them be symbols that inspire and empower you.

2. This week, once the sacred space is created, light the candle as a symbol of the spirit within you. Dedicate the day to shining that light to others.

3. Look for opportunities to transform mundane activities into meaningful rituals. For example, consider your routine shower. Water symbolizes purification. As the water pours over you, think of a fear, limiting belief, or difficult emotion being cleansed away and disappearing down the drain.

4. Be mindful of opportunities to transform the ordinary into the sacred in all your endeavors.

Deepening Joy

What I am grateful for this week

_____

_____

_____

_____

_____

_____

_____

Three things that went well this week

_____

_____

_____

_____

_____

_____

_____

Week Thirty

*I*n the play called life, happiness and fulfillment are derived from finding the script that was written just for you. You know you are playing the right part by the ease and delight with which you experience each act, by playing the part of the authentic you.

Reflecting on Joy

❀ Considering my life as a play in which I have the leading role, am I passionate and inspired by the part I am currently playing?

❀ What would be a fitting title for this play?

❀ What changes would I make to the script and my role, in order for the play to be a joyful, natural expression of who I really am?

❀ What assistance (training, coaching, mentoring) do I need to fully express the role for which I am best cast?

Activating Joy

1. In your journal, make two columns with these headings: "My Current Role" and "My Ideal Role." Under each heading, list the qualities/attributes of the persona you have been/will be playing. Give your new role full permission to be your most joyful, authentic, and creatively expressive self.

2. Look for, or create, a symbol that represents the essence of the part that is authentically YOU! Examples include: a crystal, statue, natural object or photograph. Place it in a visible space of great honor.

3. Make a collage of images that represent the life script that ignites your passion and fuels your joy.

4. Play a piece of inspiring music like "Chariots of Fire". Close your eyes. Imagine yourself playing the part of your ideal role. You may be writing, speaking, cooking, coaching, caretaking or painting. Whatever your part, act it out with enthusiasm. Feel the power as you move your body to reflect the actual motions you are engaged in as you play the part that is uniquely yours.

~ Deepening Joy ~

What I am grateful for this week

_____

_____

_____

_____

_____

_____

_____

_____

Three things that went well this week

_____

_____

_____

_____

_____

_____

_____

Week Thirty-One

An exotic vacation, a new outfit, a promotion or a flirtation yield only fleeting happiness. Lasting happiness is not dependent on the mirror, the money, or the mate! However, actively expressing *love, kindness* and *gratitude* creates the ideal inner condition for a life of lasting joy and delight.

Reflecting on Joy

❀ Where do I see evidence that lasting happiness is not guaranteed by the acquisition of things? Who or what comes to mind?

❀ When has extending love to another contributed to my ongoing joy?

❀ What would need to change for me to express more love, kindness, and gratitude?

❀ To whom will I actively express all those things, starting this week?

 *Activating Joy*

1. Make a list of five people to whom you will extend your love this week. How will you do that?

2. Make a list of five people to whom you will express gratitude this week.

3. Practice random acts of kindness this week. Be creative and have fun. Notice the impact on you and on the others.

4. Make a sticky note or other visual reminder of the three qualities to regularly practice this and every week: love, gratitude, and kindness.

~ Deepening Joy ~

What I am grateful for this week

_____
_____
_____
_____
_____
_____
_____
_____

Three things that went well this week

_____
_____
_____
_____
_____
_____
_____
_____

Week Thirty-Two

*P*erfectionism is a damaging inner demon, responsible for the mental, physical and spiritual malaise affecting vast numbers of women. Symptoms of this disease include irritability, insomnia, anxiety and depression. Perfectionism steals a woman's vitality, creativity and joy. Antidotes for the weary feminine spirit include going slowly, retreating into nature, spiritual practices, play, and, most important, kindly granting yourself permission to be human!

Reflecting on Joy

❋ Where in my life is my happiness diminished by a tendency toward perfectionism?

❋ What would I have more of/less of if I rebelled against that unattainable perfectionism?

❋ Am I ignoring an inner whisper that yearns for a simpler, slower, more balanced life—for more wonder, delight, adventure?

❋ How do I "medicate" the emotional pain that comes from the stress of trying to be a perfect woman—alcohol, food, sex, obsession with my body, compulsive "doing"?

Activating Joy

1. This week, become conscious of how perfectionism may be driving you. Record your observations in your journal.

2. Listen for the still, small voice within, who may be yearning for a change. Write about her desires.

3. Initiate a practice of saying "no," and talking back to the inner perfectionist—in work, in relationships, in your appearance, in your social life.

4. Post this quote where you can see it: *"Use what talents you possess; the woods would be very silent if no birds sang except those that sang best."* ~ Henry van Dyke

Deepening Joy

What I am grateful for this week

_____
_____
_____
_____
_____
_____
_____
_____
_____

Three things that went well this week

_____
_____
_____
_____
_____
_____
_____
_____

Week Thirty-Three

*T*reasured memories are a catalyst for happiness in the present moment. It's scientifically proven that the practice of savoring precious memories has the power to alleviate inner suffering—anger, fear, sadness and confusion—by filling the mind and heart with joy and love. Harmony and well-being are restored, as one relives past moments of happiness as though they are happening in present time.

Reflecting on Joy

❀ What memories bring me great joy from the last month, year, ten years, from childhood?

❀ Which happy memory is easiest to recall in great detail?

❀ As I recall that happy memory, how does it affect my mood?

❀ What photos or mementos activate my joy? Which one(s) will I focus on daily this week?

Activating Joy

1. Write a brief description of a memory that fills you with deep joy.

2. Do this…it works! Each day this week, sit quietly. Close your eyes. Recall a joyful memory as though you're re-living it now. Activate all five senses. Notice what you see, hear, touch, smell, taste. Feel the joy. Amplify it. Hold the feeling for 60 seconds or more.

3. Create a photo album or collage of significant joyful memories. Linger with each image, savoring the happy memory it evokes.

4. Make time to be still. With eyes closed, conjure up the face of a treasured "other." Savor the pure delight of activating your love. Next, feel the gratitude for this special being.

~ Deepening Joy ~

What I am grateful for this week

_____
_____
_____
_____
_____
_____
_____

Three things that went well this week

_____
_____
_____
_____
_____
_____
_____

Week Thirty-Four

Being stuck in a career, a relationship or a habitual behavior pattern is one of the greatest barriers to joy. Feeling like a hostage to old, outdated ways of being can feel like living out a prison sentence. Break out now. Escape to freedom. The first powerful step is to decide to step out into the light of a new beginning.

Reflecting on Joy

❋ Where in my life do I feel imprisoned (e.g., work, relationship, home)? What keeps me trapped?

❋ How would my life be different if I escaped that prison?

❋ What action(s) will I take to liberate myself?

❋ Who can support and encourage me to walk out?

Activating Joy

1. Make a promise to liberate yourself. Look in the mirror and say it out loud.

2. Write down your intention to "walk out" of "prison" and record the actions you will take this week (e.g., join a support group, hire a mentor, a career counselor, or a psychotherapist, etc.) to give form to and empower your decision.

3. Identify at least one person who can support you in finding the courage to break free. Ask for her help today.

4. Draw, paint or sculpt a symbol of the joy awaiting you on the other side. Put it in a place of honor.

Deepening Joy

What I am grateful for this week

_____

_____

_____

_____

_____

_____

_____

Three things that went well this week

_____

_____

_____

_____

_____

_____

_____

Week Thirty-Five

ristotle said, *"Happiness is up to you."* Whenever life puts unhappy, difficult people in your path, you can choose to be happy regardless of whether they're loved ones, coworkers or neighbors. To respond otherwise is to sabotage your own peace and contentment, as well as pouring kerosene on the fire of others' negativity.

# Reflecting on Joy

🌸 In my family, who have I wished to be happier so that I could be happier?

🌸 Which one of my friends or co-workers have I wished to be happier so that I could be happier?

🌸 What would change if I let go of those fantasies and radiated joy, instead of mirroring others' sour dispositions and negative behaviors?

🌸 How can I bring myself more happiness when interacting with these people, starting today?

Activating Joy

1. If you are willing, make a decision to stop depending on another person's happiness to be the source of your joy. Write that intention in your journal.

2. Tie a four-foot length of cord to a doorknob. Imagine it symbolizing the "pull" or desire you have for a specific person to be happy so that you can be happy. Pull the cord tight and feel that desire. Say out loud, *"I let go!"* Cut the cord and feel the freedom as you let go. Repeat for each person you need to release.

3. Fill your own pipeline with happiness. Deliberately activate your inner joy. Practice radiating that joy to everyone you encounter.

4. CoDA (Codependents Anonymous) and Al-Anon are 12-step programs that are powerfully effective in helping people to lovingly detach in order to maintain well-being. Find meetings and information online.

~ Deepening Joy ~

What I am grateful for this week

_____
_____
_____
_____
_____
_____
_____
_____

Three things that went well this week

_____
_____
_____
_____
_____
_____
_____
_____

Week Thirty-Six

*I*magine the inner strength and determination it took for Anne Frank to revive her happiness and to speak the following words: *"My advice is: go outside to the fields, enjoy nature and sunshine. Go out and try to recapture happiness in yourself and in God. Think of all the beauty that's still left in and around you and be happy."* Being in nature—especially in solitude—reawakens joy, wonder, and inner peace.

Reflecting on Joy

❀ If Anne Frank was able to recapture her happiness by remembering the beauty of nature, what inner disturbance or present difficulty could I transform by following her advice?

❀ Am I willing to make time to be in nature, in solitude, to transform my challenges through the joy I find there?

❀ What habit would I have to let go of (TV, phone calls, Internet surfing) to make time for mini-retreats into nature?

❀ What special place in nature will I visit this week?

 *Activating Joy*

1. Let this week be devoted to recapturing your inner peace and joy in nature. Take daily ten-minute breaks outside to refresh your spirit.

2. Schedule a day to enjoy a delightful nature spot (the ocean, a forest, a park, a lake, a river or a mountain) to enhance clarity, creativity, and problem-solving.

3. Look for "teachers" in nature. Carefully observe the creatures you see. Notice their beauty and their behaviors. What can you learn from them?

4. Watch for solutions to reveal themselves in the face of a flower, the flight of a bird, the pace of a snail. Record your observations.

Deepening Joy

What I am grateful for this week

_____

_____

_____

_____

_____

_____

_____

_____

Three things that went well this week

_____

_____

_____

_____

_____

_____

_____

Week Thirty-Seven

It is an evolutionary fact that the human brain is hardwired to be cautious and fearful because, once upon a time, our survival depended on it. Unless we are being chased by a tiger or facing another life-threatening circumstance, the cause of fear doesn't actually exist in the present moment. Fear is an illusion: *False Evidence Appearing Real*. Fear suffocates joy. The antidote to fear is rightful action! Silent era actress, Dorothy Bernard said, *"Courage is fear that's said its prayers"*.

 *Reflecting on Joy*

❋ When has my zest for life been dampened by fear?

❋ What inspiring life dreams were thwarted by fear, and what was I afraid of?

❋ What passion within is currently suffocating underneath my fears?

❋ What desire would I initiate today if I had no fear? What inner qualities would help me banish the fear?

 *Activating Joy*

1. Light a candle and sit quietly, asking yourself the question, *"What would I do if I had no fear?"*

2. In your journal, record your reflections from #1. Next, make three columns with the headings: My Desire, What I Fear, Challenging the Fear.

3. Choose 1–3 primary desires that are currently held hostage by fear and list them in column 1. Next to each, in column 2 record the fears that keep you stuck. In column 3, talk back to the fears like a tough trial attorney. Prove them wrong!

4. Create a ritual that engages your unconscious mind in support of banishing fear. With a hunk of clay, sculpt a symbol of your fear—(for example: *"I'll fail"*; *"I'll lose my friends…they'll ridicule me"*). Radiate the fearful feeling into the clay. Once complete, with fierce determination to release it, smash the sculpture and release the fear.

5. Decide to take action on your desire. Define the action steps you will take this week, over the next month, the next six months.

Deepening Joy

What I am grateful for this week

_____

_____

_____

_____

_____

_____

_____

_____

Three things that went well this week

_____

_____

_____

_____

_____

_____

_____

Week Thirty-Eight

Positive thinking is a tonic for the brain. Research shows that as you learn how to activate positive emotions, regardless of external circumstances, you rejuvenate and stimulate the brain. The benefits include increased concentration, clarity and creativity. A brain nourished by positive thinking and joy is a ticket to effectiveness, fulfillment and true success.

 *Reflecting on Joy*

❋ What in my life am I holding in a negative light?

❋ When I think about that issue, how do I feel (e.g., sad, angry, resentful, jealous, fearful)?

❋ Knowing that these feelings are compromising my brain function, how am I willing to change my attitude toward this issue?

❋ How does it feel when I hold the positive belief that in all challenges—even this one—there is an opportunity waiting to be born?

Activating Joy

1. Consider a challenge in your life. Ask yourself what possible opportunities could emerge from this challenge. Write them down to plant mental seeds for "possibility thinking."

2. Upon awakening each morning, speak this affirmation: *"I am calm, as I allow unexpected opportunity to arise from challenging circumstances."*

3. Practice optimism. Visualize the best possible outcome for this situation. Decide it's possible! Act as if you believe in it. Fake it until you make it!

4. In great detail, paint a picture of yourself in your mind, "celebrating" this positive outcome with joy. Repeat daily. Envision this daily, deepening the positive feelings that result.

Deepening Joy

What I am grateful for this week

_____
_____
_____
_____
_____
_____
_____
_____

Three things that went well this week

_____
_____
_____
_____
_____
_____
_____
_____

Week Thirty-Nine

*A*ncient Hawaiian teachings encourage the practice of actively blessing all the good in life. While similar to expressing gratitude, the act of blessing your loved one, your home, your car, your work, or your miraculous body can become a joyful ritual of love and deep appreciation. Remember that what you appreciate appreciates!

 *Reflecting on Joy*

✤ How often do I stop to appreciate and bless all the good in my life? In the world?

✤ What issues, thoughts, behaviors or emotions overshadow the acknowledgment for all the blessings in my life?

✤ What relationship or aspects of my life could be improved by focusing on the good, rather than on what I think is not working?

✤ If I were an announcer on "Good News TV", what would I be reporting about my life/the world?

Activating Joy

1. Draw a big pie chart with eight sections. Label them: Career; Friends; Family; Health; Recreation; Personal Growth; Finances; Spirituality. In each section, write phrases describing all the wonderful aspects of that part of your life.

2. For each category above, make a list of actions you can take to experience even more appreciation and fulfillment. Record them in your journal.

3. Write down five blessings in your life/the world.

4. Each night this week, before you go to sleep, pause to reflect on all the good you witnessed today. Bless one thing in your life and one thing in the world.

~ Deepening Joy ~

What I am grateful for this week

_____
_____
_____
_____
_____
_____
_____
_____

Three things that went well this week

_____
_____
_____
_____
_____
_____
_____

Week Forty

aughter is a miracle drug—a powerful antidote to the anxiety, depression and dis-ease that too many people suffer in this era of high-speed, 24/7, achievement-oriented lifestyles. Laughter is free therapy. It strengthens the immune system, restores vitality, and boosts happiness. Laughter is a good prescription for sustaining the spirit in these frantic, challenging times. Laughter opens the gates of enthusiasm, creativity, and fresh perspectives on life issues.

Reflecting on Joy

✦ Looking back on my childhood, was there laughter in my home?

✦ Who or what was considered funny in my childhood home, and do I consider funny today?

✦ Who or what inspires my laughter today?

✦ How might my life be impacted by prioritizing laughter?

Activating Joy

1. This week, pay attention to how often you laugh. Laugh more, and make others laugh.

2. What thoughts, moods or issues could be "cracked open" by simply "cracking up"? This week, practice laughing out loud at perceived challenges as they arise. Take yourself less seriously.

3. Go online and research "Laughter Yoga." Find a group near you. Attend a session. Women LOVE the experience.

4. Start a laughter project this week: collect jokes, rent funny movies, read books that make you laugh out loud, and search *www.youtube.com* for funny videos—free entertainment in the comfort of your home!

Deepening Joy

What I am grateful for this week

_____

_____

_____

_____

_____

_____

_____

_____

Three things that went well this week

_____

_____

_____

_____

_____

_____

_____

Week Forty-One

Taking pleasure in material possessions is a part of the human experience, especially in the comparatively affluent Western world. When such pleasures result in a compulsive quest for more, more, more, the aliveness and richness of the spirit are corrupted. Living in harmony with your "true nature" is the essential key to a truly prosperous and happy life.

Reflecting on Joy

✤ What is my "true nature?" What am I like when I am really being me?

✤ Being completely honest, what external "stuff"—possessions, titles, privileges—give me a sense of self-worth, power, success?

✤ How have I been influenced into believing that wealth, prestige, and possessions are the source of my happiness?

✤ What is a project, a career, or a challenge that aligns with my authentic self, that would fill me with such intense joy and inspiration that the importance of my "stuff" would pale in comparison to my fulfillment?

Activating Joy

1. Sit quietly and reflect on who you really are—your "true nature."

2. Next, reflect on what you value in life that is not an external possession or role.

3. Without blame or judgment, write about how you are using your time and energy in support of material things you could possibly do, even thrive, without.

4. Write each possession on a stone with a marker, whether it's the luxury car, the jewelry, the high-definition TV or the impressive title. Feel your willingness, or not, to release each one. If you're willing, throw the stone as hard and far as you can. Notice your experience. Do you feel lighter?

~ Deepening Joy ~

What I am grateful for this week

_____
_____
_____
_____
_____
_____
_____
_____

Three things that went well this week

_____
_____
_____
_____
_____
_____
_____
_____

Week Forty-Two

Dolphins are ambassadors of joy! In the presence of dolphins, humans have reported a transcendent experience of euphoria, a dissolving of fear and stuck patterns, as well as a lightening of anxiety and depression. From the Ancient Greek philosophers to contemporary psychologists, neuroscientists, and biochemists, the astonishing emotional and physical healing influence of dolphins has been researched and documented. As an antidote to the dis-ease of stress, fatigue, and listlessness, we can benefit from modeling our lives after these magnificent creatures. Your dolphin-like life would be characterized by curiosity, fun and games, nurturing, gentleness, love and compassion for even the difficult people, helping those in distress, healing with sound, and, above all, community. Dive into an ocean of joy as you invite the "dolphin spirit" into your life!

Reflecting on Joy

❋ What dolphin-like qualities are prominent in my life today? Not prominent?

❋ Which dolphin characteristics would benefit my work, relationships, and overall well-being?

❋ What would change in my life/work if I adopted the above qualities? If I were to create a joy-enhancing community, whom would I include? What could our common purpose be (e.g., to have more fun; to adopt a project for the common good)?

❋ What belief or attitude would I need to release to empower this commitment?

Activating Joy

1. Dedicate this week to playfulness and fun. Make a "play-date" with favorite friends (e.g., a game night; a movie or stand-up comedy night; a Karaoke event). Schedule it within the next two weeks. Repeat often for best results!

2. Practice the feminine principle of deep nurturing this week, starting with you! Schedule a time to nurture yourself and one other person this week. Repeat weekly and watch your joy rise!

3. Take five-to-ten-minute breaks this week to watch dolphin videos on *www.youtube.com*. In the search box enter "scuba diving with dolphins"; "wild dolphins yelling at me"; "dolphin play bubble ring." (Even watching films of dolphins can alleviate anxiety and depression.)

4. Calm the mind and open the heart with music and dolphins. Upon awakening and before sleep, deeply relax with the following selections from *www.youtube.com*. Search for: "dolphins—a short meditation"; "whales, dolphins and chakras"; "Medwyn Goodall—dolphin companion." Notice the impact on your body, mind and spirit. Create a daily practice of such experiences to deepen your inner peace and joy.

Deepening Joy

What I am grateful for this week

_____

_____

_____

_____

_____

_____

_____

Three things that went well this week

_____

_____

_____

_____

_____

_____

_____

Week Forty-Three

*T*he simple pursuit of *pleasure* is no guarantee of lasting happiness. Three essential elements of a consistently joyful life journey are ***meaning, purpose*** and ***inspiration***. The pleasure derived from the pursuit of those qualities ensures fulfillment and joy.

Reflecting on Joy

✽ What do I devote time to in my life that brings momentary pleasure, but has no lasting meaning?

✽ Am I willing to let go of any of these activities?

✽ What do I spend time on that may be purposeful and meaningful, but not pleasurable for me?

✽ What is an experience that brings me both pleasure and a sense of meaningful purpose?

✽ What would change if I eliminated the purposeful activities that don't give me pleasure, or transformed them with a positive attitude?

Activating Joy

1. Do an awareness inventory. In your journal, make three columns with the headings: Pleasure, Meaning, Pleasure and Meaning.

2. In each column, list activities that are purely pleasurable, purely meaningful, and both pleasurable and meaningful.

3. Based on your lists, consider what changes would bring you more joy. What will you change this week?

4. Schedule time for two activities this week that are pleasurable and meaningful. Repeat consistently, on a weekly basis.

Deepening Joy

What I am grateful for this week

_____
_____
_____
_____
_____
_____
_____
_____

Three things that went well this week

_____
_____
_____
_____
_____
_____
_____
_____

Week Forty-Four

The human body is an astonishing and miraculous gift. Accepting, praising, and loving the body—exactly as it is—opens a channel to contentment. We must each find ways to nurture, nourish, and rejoice in our bodies, for they are the vehicles for all sensuality, creativity, inspiration and adventure. They are the temples of our souls.

Reflecting on Joy

❀ What is my relationship to my body? What thoughts and feelings do I subliminally suggest to my body?

❀ How are my attitudes toward my body influenced by other people? By the media?

❀ What would it be like to rebel, to reject the media's messages that I need to look younger, thinner, and more beautiful?

❀ Who could I align with for support and encouragement to successfully extinguish media-influenced body perfectionism—a friend, a women's circle?

Activating Joy

1. Dedicate this week to a "love fest" for your body. In your journal, write about all the wonderful things your body has made possible for you. Include all parts of your body, including the musculoskeletal system, organs, limbs and the five senses.

2. When awakening, stay in bed and perform a five-minute gratitude ritual for your amazing body. Starting at the top of your head, gently place the palms of your hands over a body part: skull/brain; eyes; ears; lips, throat; heart, and so on. Feel deep appreciation for how it has served you since birth.

3. This week, plan something that activates joy while nurturing your body. Dancing, singing, biking, hiking and yoga are just a few examples.

4. Invite women friends to a "love fest" for the body. Sitting in a circle, light a candle and pass a bowl of soil. Have each woman bury a stone representing a release of a negative belief about her body. Celebrate with wholesome foods. End with a "show and tell." Share ideas and resources for healing, nurturing and just plain fun (e.g., favorite cosmetics, skilled massage therapists, juicing recipes—the sky's the limit!)

Deepening Joy

What I am grateful for this week

_____

_____

_____

_____

_____

_____

_____

_____

Three things that went well this week

_____

_____

_____

_____

_____

_____

_____

_____

Week Forty-Five

We are the transformers we've been waiting for. As women with five-plus decades of living, learning, growing, and mothering—children, gardens, projects or businesses—we hold the key to personal and planetary healing. Our caring and our love are the antidotes to the dis-ease and spiritual malaise of our times—locally and globally. As we offer our time, our attention, and our nurturing to the needs of our human community and of Mother Earth, our deep joy and fulfillment sends ripples far and wide.

Reflecting on Joy

✻ Knowing that my capacity to extend love is dependent upon my self-love, how can I increase my self-respect and nurturing at this time?

✻ What three specific actions can I take to increase my self-nurturing?

✻ How might it impact the lives of others if I were on a mission of radiating love and compassion to everyone I encounter?

✻ As I consider the dis-ease and needs of Mother Earth, how can I extend my caring and love in support of her healing?

Activating Joy

1. In your journal, record your thoughts and feelings in response to the questions above.

2. Sitting quietly with your eyes closed, send love, forgiveness and compassion to your heart. Really feel it. From your heart center, radiate a colorful beam of love light throughout your home, neighborhood, state, and to places of suffering around the world.

3. In addition to repeating #2 as a daily practice, make it your "mission" to be a "love magnet" wherever you go! The more love you extend, the more love you magnetize.

4. To make your life a living legacy to the planet, become actively involved with a community or organization dedicated to planetary healing (e.g., Pachamama Alliance: *www.pachamama.org*)

Deepening Joy

What I am grateful for this week

_____
_____
_____
_____
_____
_____
_____
_____

Three things that went well this week

_____
_____
_____
_____
_____
_____
_____

Week Forty-Six

True happiness cannot be found by building a life or a career based on anyone else's idea about who you should be or how you should live. Joy takes root when you know what your unique natural gift is, then design your work and life around it. Whether your gift is lovingly grandparenting, writing a novel, launching a new business, fund-raising to save polar bears, or empowering women and girls around the world, follow your heart and you will soar.

Reflecting on Joy

- Do I know what my unique gift is—so natural, it's like breathing?

- How would I describe my unique talent/gift? Am I actively using it in my life/work?

- How have I been influenced by other ideas of what, how, or who I should be? How have parents, siblings, friends, society, the media influenced my choices in life/work?

- What is one action that would free me to more fully express my natural gifts in my life/work?

Activating Joy

1. Imagine your best friend, mentor, higher self, ancestor, angel or wise woman, looking at you with love and compassion.

2. In quiet meditation, ask this being: "What gift was I born to offer the world? What unique contribution will bring me peace and fulfillment at the end of my life?" Listen intently for words, images, and/or an intuitive sense. Record your insights.

3. Create (draw, paint, sculpt) a concrete symbol of a unique innate gift. Place it in a prominent place. Honor it.

4. Write 3–5 action steps you will complete in the next 30 days that will initiate the intention to offer your gift to the world. Record them on your calendar.

Deepening Joy

What I am grateful for this week

_____
_____
_____
_____
_____
_____
_____
_____

Three things that went well this week

_____
_____
_____
_____
_____
_____
_____
_____

Week Forty-Seven

"*H*ere's to women. Happiness and joy of life to all of us!*" proclaims Evelyne Boren, internationally acclaimed impressionist, watercolorist, and oil painter. Evelyne suffered great fear and loss as a child during World War II in Germany. Nevertheless, her intentional joie de vivre is revealed in her art and in the following expression: *"My life started with the war. Because of that experience, I have always sought out happiness and peace. I suppose, subconsciously, this is the reason I create cheerful paintings."*

 *Reflecting on Joy*

✤ What painful episodes from childhood may be damp-ening my joy today?

✤ How can I seek lasting happiness and peace, despite the past?

✤ What activities, attitudes and relationships can help me overcome past hurt or loss?

✤ Who do I need to forgive to free myself from the past and enjoy inner peace today?

 *Activating Joy*

1. Go to *www.evelyneboren.com*. Notice how the beauty of Evelyne's paintings affects your mood. You may want to treat yourself to the book, *Evelyne Boren: Joie de Vivre* by Suzanne Deats. You will discover joyous art throughout!

2. Identify a creative endeavor, project or activity that imbues you with a sense of joy and peace. This week, do something every day to engage with it.

3. Imagine a guardian angel whose love transforms all past burdens. Write a loving letter from that angel to the vulnerable child inside you.

4. Connie would like to hear about the joy-enhancing projects that have helped you overcome past adversity, fear, or depression. Please send one paragraph describing the project or work that has empowered your joy, in spite of painful past experiences to *connie@joyafterfifty.com*.

~ Deepening Joy ~

What I am grateful for this week

_____
_____
_____
_____
_____
_____
_____
_____

Three things that went well this week

_____
_____
_____
_____
_____
_____
_____

Week Forty-Eight

"*Things won are done; joy's soul lies in the doing.*" Consider the relevance of Shakespeare's quote to your life. Remember the delight you've known in the process of reaching your heartfelt goals. Today, we know that the joy is in the journey. It lies on the path to reaching meaningful goals that are based on our values.

Reflecting on Joy

❈ What projects and goals am I engaged in at the present time?

❈ Are they "self-concordant" goals that have meaning to me now and are in alignment with my values?

❈ If they are not self-concordant goals, why did I decide to pursue them?

❈ Am I ready to search my soul for what has meaning for me today, and to consider taking an alternate path?

 *Activating Joy*

1. Take a walk or sit quietly and ask yourself, "Am I following the path I am presently on with a light step and a joyful heart?"

2. If so, give thanks and take pleasure in each day's journey. If not, imagine a path that might lead to harmony, fulfillment and joy.

3. In your journal, write what a "perfect" day might look and feel like if your feet were planted fully on your chosen path.

4. Invite 6–10 friends for a "brain exchange." Sit in a circle. Each woman asks the group for creative strategies toward the successful outcome of her goal. For three minutes, the group brainstorms nonstop, without censoring creative ideas. One person types the ideas up to be e-mailed later. This is really fun and amazingly powerful!

Deepening Joy

What I am grateful for this week

_____

_____

_____

_____

_____

_____

_____

Three things that went well this week

_____

_____

_____

_____

_____

_____

_____

Week Forty-Nine

*J*oy is an inner resource that is impervious to the judgments of others—child, spouse, boss, coworker or neighbor. Regardless of other people's opinions of you, happiness is a choice you make, one moment at a time. Eleanor Roosevelt spoke to this fact when she said, *"No one can make you feel inferior without your consent."* No one can make you feel any emotion without your consent.

Reflecting on Joy

※ Am I determined to choose happiness in spite of others' assessments of me?

※ Whose opinions of me have I allowed to "stick"? How has that affected my happiness?

※ Even though it may feel like a tall order, what benefits might I enjoy by refusing to allow my happiness to be compromised by others' judgments of me?

※ What creative ideas would help me remain "whole" and happy when others are not?

Activating Joy

1. Make three columns for your answers to these questions. Record your answers:
   a. Whose opinion of me have I allowed to disturb my inner peace? Make a list of names.
   b. What emotion(s) arises in me in reaction to this person's opinion of me?
   c. How has my response to this person's judgments interfered with my optimal functioning?

2. Make a list of creative solutions to ensure your joy and well-being in response to another person's criticism (e.g., ending the conversation, going for a walk, calling a friend for support, sending yourself love and compassion).

3. This week, practice the following joy boosters:
   a. Pause when you feel agitated. Take time out to be calm before and after communicating with critical people.
   b. Communicate calmly and assertively to such people that it is not okay for them to criticize you.

4. To counteract the effects of external judgments, make a list of what your friends love and admire about you. Read it daily. Look in the mirror and say, *"I Love You."*

Deepening Joy

What I am grateful for this week

_____
_____
_____
_____
_____
_____
_____
_____

Three things that went well this week

_____
_____
_____
_____
_____
_____
_____
_____

Week Fifty

There is great wisdom in patiently waiting for the clarity that reveals the appropriate action for you to take on significant life issues. An abiding inner peace comes to those who trust that a higher intelligence will reveal a beautiful solution or direction to follow—not by our timetable, but by life's timetable.

 *Reflecting on Joy*

✳ In retrospect, when did I struggle with an issue or decision that later resolved itself gracefully?

✳ What issue am I facing today that is as yet unresolved?

✳ What thoughts, feelings or judgments have arisen regarding this situation?

✳ What would change if I decided to surrender my will and wait patiently for the wisdom of the universe to reveal the right action for me to take?

Activating Joy

1. This week, decide to be patient, trusting and content, regardless of the lack of clarity around a significant life situation.

2. Experiment with the act of letting go. Decorate a shoebox and label it *"What I can't, life can!"* Write down the issue you are going to turn over to a greater wisdom. With deliberate intention, release it into the shoebox.

3. Each morning this week, reinforce your intention of letting go. Close your eyes. On the out-breath, silently say, *"I breathe out control and attachment."* On the in-breath, mentally affirm, *"I breathe in trust."* Repeat four times.

4. To reinforce your trust that everything IS in divine order, write and recite the following affirmation in the morning and before sleep: *"As I embrace each moment with trust, my life unfolds in perfect harmony with ease, grace and joy."*

~ Deepening Joy ~

What I am grateful for this week

_____
_____
_____
_____
_____
_____
_____
_____

Three things that went well this week

_____
_____
_____
_____
_____
_____
_____

Week Fifty-One

*D*eep fulfillment and joy come to those who are in service to a "cause" beyond personal and professional goals. Women 50+ could rock the world back onto an axis of caring, love, and generosity, if we each "adopted" a cause with a commitment of energy, time, and dedication. Leaving footprints on the hearts of those in need is a living legacy to the world.

Reflecting on Joy

✤ When did I serve a "cause" that enhanced my happiness?

✤ How am I inspired to be of service to the greater human community at this time?

✤ What specific global causes am I inspired to support by giving time, energy, and/or financial aid?

✤ What actions will I take this week to "adopt" a cause?

Activating Joy

1. Research those causes that inspire you. "Google" organizations like Heifer International; Doctors Without Borders; Habitat for Humanity; St. Jude Children's Hospital; and Sammy Rides.

2. Decide how you can be of service to one special cause that inspires you. This week, decide how you will get involved and lend your support to that cause. Take one action now.

3. Initiate a "cause" of lifting the spirits of the people you encounter daily. Offer your full presence and warmth to the bank teller, barista, or grocery checker.

4. List five people whose joy you will enhance by reaching out to them this week by phone or e-mail.

~ Deepening Joy ~

What I am grateful for this week

Three things that went well this week

Week Fifty-Two

*C*ongratulations! You have reached the last week of the *Joy after Fifty* program. It's possible that, as you master the art of activating joy, a new life dream may be emerging. What music is still within you? What future vision is waiting to be born? By continuing to prioritize joy, you will discover the passion and confidence to launch the life of your dreams! This is what you came here for—to shine your light into the world by joyfully living your dreams!

Reflecting on Joy

❀ Being completely honest with myself, what is the one dream—simple or life-challenging—that I most desire to manifest at this time?

❀ What do I want to experience, attain, or create so that I can say, "mission accomplished" at the end of my life?

❀ When I visualize this dream as though it's already happening, how do I feel?

❀ Knowing that people rarely reach their dreams without the support of friends and professionals, who would make up my "dream team"?

Activating Joy

1. Make time to be quiet. Light a candle and ask yourself, "What music is still within me?" "What new dream is waiting to be born?" Make notes in your journal.

2. Write down all the blocks that have inhibited or could inhibit the manifestation of your dream. Activate your fierce intention to banish them. Ask a bigger force, higher power, or ancestor to support you in releasing these obstacles. Burn them with determination. Give thanks. Feel the freedom to move ahead with joy.

3. Commit fully, trusting that with support, you will realize your dream. Write down your commitment and the date by which you will be living it. Create a collage of photos that represent your dream. Look at it daily.

4. Make a list of all the actions and steps required to manifest your dream. Give them all "by when" dates. Schedule them in your daily, weekly, monthly calendar. To ensure success, hire a mentor or coach. You can do this! Just commit and the magic begins—and never, ever give up on your dream!

I wish you a life-long journey of deep and lasting joy.
It would be my greatest pleasure to support you on your way.

With loving blessings,
Connie

About the Author

*S*ince 1986, Connie Clark, known as "America's Joy Doctor," has been a licensed psychotherapist and highly acclaimed leader of personal and professional transformation programs—as a speaker, seminar and retreat leader, and life-enhancement consultant. She empowers women with essential life skills for flourishing in fast-paced, challenging times.

Connie is recognized internationally for her dynamic and inspiring style, which has been a catalyst for hundreds of clients, helping them move from mere glimpses of desired change to breakthrough experiences. Her clients include CEOs, entrepreneurs, physicians, artists, authors, grandmothers, and women "starting over" after the empty nest, the divorce, and other major life changes.

Having reinvented her career path four times—from educator to sales manager and consultant, to psychotherapist, to speaker and author—Connie is truly an expert in supporting women's successful life/work transitions that are in alignment with their true natures, especially in the second half of life.

In 2003, she founded JoyWorks™, which incorporates empowerment seminars and conferences for women;

mastermind groups; tele-classes; and transformational *"Spa for the Spirit"* women's retreats in the U.S. and Mexico. In order to keep each woman's inspiration alive after the retreats, she provides ongoing "tele-circles" that deepen their connections to one another and to their inner callings.

Connie followed her own joy and inner calling as a co-founder of Shenoa, a retreat and learning center in Northern California, which was inspired by her association with the Findhorn Community in Scotland. For twelve years, she developed programs, served on the board of directors, and designed group experiences as the facilitator of "spiritual sustainability."

The mission of Connie's most recent project, *www.joy afterfifty.com,* is to awaken the joy within women 50+ and to encourage them to answer the important question, *"How must I live today in order to ensure deep fulfillment and peace at this stage of my life?"* She gently guides women toward defining the path that is uniquely designed to bring them lasting joy and fulfillment.

What makes Connie's heart sing: her friends and family; traveling; leading women's retreats; designing "rites of passage" for girls and women; swimming with wild dolphins; renewing awe and delight in nature; music; dancing; Kirtan (look it up!) with Jai Uttal and Krishna Das; and collaborating with like-spirited people to make a difference on the planet. Toward that end, she is proud to be involved with the projects of the Pachamama Alliance—dedicated to social justice, environmental sustainability and spiritual fulfillment.

MORE JOY AFTER FIFTY

We all need consistent support, encouragement, information and effective life skills to ensure that our days are filled with ease, happiness, passion, and meaning as we age.

Connie Clark is dedicated to enriching your life with a variety of ongoing resources to nurture and empower your joy, well-being and fulfillment—to ensure that the rest of your life is truly the best of your life!

~~~~~~~~~~~~~~~~~~~~~~~~~~~~~~~~~~

Claim a *FREE GIFT* that's waiting for you at *www.joyafterfifty.com.* **Simply enter your name and email address to receive your gift.**

In addition to your gift, you will also receive the *Joy After Fifty* newsletter and blog: tools, tips, inspiration and announcements of events and experiences and more, including:

- **Women's Retreats:** Life-transforming vacations you'll never forget
- **Teleseminars:** Topics include research on: happiness, health, longevity, love and life fulfillment. Call in and simply listen or join the discussion.
- **Audio and Video Interviews** with experts on all aspects of flourishing 50+
- **Connie's Live One Day Seminars** in the U.S. and Mexico
- **Joy after Fifty Mentoring:** Expert life-enhancement coaching—on the phone from your home or office

~~~~~~~~~~~~~~~~~~~~~~~~~~~~~~~~~

For more information, call 1-800-996-4006 or email *connie@joyafterfifty.com*

www.joyafterfifty.com
www.connieclarkjoyworks.com
www.facebook.com/joyafterfifty
www.twitter.com/joyafterfifty

Made in the USA
Charleston, SC
27 September 2011